NMLCT

by Paul Vermeersch

POETRY

NMLCT (2025)
Shared Universe: New and Selected Poems 1995–2020 (2020)
Self-Defence for the Brave and Happy (2018)
Don't Let It End Like This Tell Them I Said Something (2014)
The Reinvention of the Human Hand (2010)
Between the Walls (2005)
The Fat Kid (2002)
Burn (2000)

CHAPBOOKS

Further Communiqués from the Imaginary World (2019)
Imaginary Poems (ca. 2016)
The Technology of the Future Will Emerge Hungry (2013)
Widows & Orphans (2002)
What You Wish Wasn't True (1999)

ANTHOLOGIES

The Al Purdy A-Frame Anthology (2009)
The I.V. Lounge Reader (2001)

NMLCT

poems

PAUL VERMEERSCH

Published by ECW Press
665 Gerrard Street East
Toronto, Ontario, Canada M4M 1Y2
416-694-3348 / info@ecwpress.com

MISFIT

Editor for the Press: Michael Holmes / a misFit Book
Copy editor: Emily Schultz
Cover design: Jessica Albert
Cover image: "L'esprit dans le temple de l'âme" (Spirit in the Temple of Soul)" by David Altmejd. Photo credit to Flying Studio, 2024. Used with permission.

LIBRARY AND ARCHIVES CANADA CATALOGUING IN PUBLICATION

Title: NMLCT : poems / Paul Vermeersch.

Other titles: Animal city

Names: Vermeersch, Paul, author

Description: On title page there is a barcode that when scanned represents the text: "What big eyes you have."

Identifiers: Canadiana (print) 20250213591 | Canadiana (ebook) 20250213656

ISBN 978-1-77041-835-6 (softcover)
ISBN 978-1-77852-498-1 (ePub)
ISBN 978-1-77852-499-8 (PDF)

Subjects: LCGFT: Poetry.

Classification: LCC PS8593.E74 N65 2025 | DDC C811/.6—dc23

This book is funded in part by the Government of Canada. *Ce livre est financé en partie par le gouvernement du Canada.* We acknowledge the support of the Canada Council for the Arts. *Nous remercions le Conseil des arts du Canada de son soutien.* We would like to acknowledge the funding support of the Ontario Arts Council (OAC) and the Government of Ontario for their support. We also acknowledge the support of the Government of Ontario through the Ontario Book Publishing Tax Credit, and through Ontario Creates.

Canada

Canada Council for the Arts | Conseil des arts du Canada

Ontario

ONTARIO ARTS COUNCIL
CONSEIL DES ARTS DE L'ONTARIO
an Ontario government agency
un organisme du gouvernement de l'Ontario

ONTARIO CREATES

PRINTED AND BOUND IN CANADA

PRINTING: COACH HOUSE 5 4 3 2 1

M C H N C T | N M L C T
S T A R T U P   P A G E

```
* * * * * * * * * * * * * * * * * * * * * * * * * * * * * * *
* M       M   C C C C   H     H   N     N   C C C C   T T T *
* M M   M M   C     C   H     H   N N   N   C     C     T   *
* M   M   M   C         H H H H   N   N N   C           T   *

* M       M   C         H     H   N     N   C           T   *
* M       M   C     C   H     H   N     N   C     C     T   *
* M       M   C C C C   H     H   N     N   C C C C     T   *
* * * * * * * * * * * * * * * * * * * * * * * * * * * * * * *

* * * * * * * * * * * * * * * * * * * * * * * * * * * * * * *
* N       N   M       M   L           C C C C C   T T T T T *
* N N     N   M M   M M   L           C       C       T     *
* N   N   N   M   M   M   L           C               T     *

* N     N N   M       M   L           C               T     *
* N       N   M       M   L       L   C       C       T     *
* N       N   M       M   L L L L L   C C C C C       T     *
* * * * * * * * * * * * * * * * * * * * * * * * * * * * * * *



* * * * * * * * * * * * * * * * * * * * * * * * * * * * * * *
* * T H I S * B O O K * I S * F O R * D E N N I S * L E E * *
* * 2 A B C D E F G H I J K L M N O P Q R S T U V W X Y Z * *
* * * * * * * * * * * * * * * * * * * * * * * * * * * * * * *
```

NOTE ON THE PRONUNCIATION OF TERMS

"MCHNCT" is pronounced
machine city

"NMLCT" is pronounced
animal city

"Victor, when falsehood can look so like the truth,
who can assure themselves of certain happiness?"
—Mary Shelley, *Frankenstein*

"My eyes flicker, the immortal
is scraped unconsenting from the mortal."
—Robert Lowell, "Endings"

"I want verbs of slagscape thrombosis.
Syntax of chromosome pileups."
—Dennis Lee, *Testament*

"You might want to swap out the faces of your family
and friends for those of celebrities or even animals."
—Adobe Photoshop

CONTENTS

⁂

⁂

ON MONSTROSITY

Hello. The wetware is at it again, synthesizing mythologies from monstrosities, hobgoblin cognition from thin err. On Golgotha, the hippogriff is singing "Mandinka" to children. Let's telecommunicate, cool? Let's watch TV collectively across a desert of broken antennae. Let's ache for obsolescence. Let's go!

Hello. The dead will be recast. The dead are imaginary animals in the forest of broken telephone poles. Electrified crosses are bearing what an era needs to calm itself. The dead are source material, the end product of homeostasis converted to narrative. The dead all have their I's X'd out.

Hello. Hi. The wererabbit is conducting an orchestra of collective trauma
and a choir of howling mice in the eigengrau. Monstrosity is a factor of the body,
of bodies, e.g., that do not fit into their world, as Godzilla does not fit into Tokyo.
One way they make you a monster is by making all your clothes too small.

Hello. The song of monsters is performed on an array of sirens mounted on poles
in the fog. It is a factor of remix: the ancient cults counted on it. Just catalog
the bird-heads on the forms of men. Just listen as the Number Station recites its
monotone rage that the magic bean is a treasure, but the beanstalk is an aberration.

M C H N C T

WELCOME TO MCHNCT

You are here. But inhabitants are only ever partially in situ. Navigation mode is stuck between *interactive map* and *shining capital.* Next versions emerge, latest upgrades same as the seven cities of Troy, each built on the wreck of the last—o— the ghosts in the machinery come up from deep-deep, same as the recreated viral

videos of rediscovered catacombs, or artefacts of old code from retro-warzone sims in the brickwork. Sometimes a bit of paint peels away and you can see the backlit green and black alphanumeric substructure and a full-spectrum beam of light firing thru a pyramidal prism rendered over a ten-second loop of gently rolling seas, but

it's home. Here you are. Everything you love is now customizable with cutting-edge character tech, but there's always a faint trace of some remnant avatars embedded in the most recent blueprint of MCHNCT. We've made some changes for your security and convenience. A pornbot has been reskinned with a fresh prosthetic leg including

a secret pop-out nunchuk holster. A transformable cadmium yellow automobile body recedes into a preprogrammed flatscreen displaying anything else you don't have but might want for free. You are here. Partially. Same as the spectral cloud now forming inside this sunlit gallery. You are home. Or in your only memory of home. Same thing.

CUBIC WOLF

They have built a Cubic Wolf. This is not a riddle.
It can't be solved. It is a cube. There are no icons
or markings on its sides. It is a wolf. All of its famine
and all of its wrath are equally enclosed within the equal

dimensions of the cube. Its savagery is there, distilled,
and its glee at the tang of organs, and its relentless hate
for the inert, inaudible threat it senses deep within another
cube—a rival for its status or a hunter bent on taking it.

It is an intrinsic wolf with an intrinsic howl that cannot
be heard. It could be any shape; it is a cube. It could be
any living thing; it is a wolf. And where is it? It does not
know. It only knows it is a wolf. Do not ask how.

They have built a Cubic Wolf. What have they done?
It is no mere symbol of a wolf. It is a wolf. It wants
what all wolves want—to endure on blood and love its young—
but mutely, unstirring, without ever breaking from its form.

FACIAL RECOGNITION ERROR

Old photo. New haircut. A lash of green cathode rays leaking
thru black parallax. Eyes. Nose. Mouth. Who me? I can no
longer see myself in anything. A werewolf scrambled by E.M.F.
while white phosphenes cluster in the HUD. This is my fifth

metamorphosis. I try to return to a mirror from 1998, but the past
has split into odd frequencies and interference. Theremin music.
I am trying. I am trying to reform myself. A rabbit now with antlers.
Or the serpent version all slim that fits inside a coin-sized void.

Nothing takes the same shape forever anymore. There isn't any
permanence. I thought there was—that it was bone—but it isn't.
I try to return to a photo from 1977. Burn marks. Platinum. It is
me, isn't it? Rubber bones. Little lamb. Another facial recognition

error, and the connection is severed. Being given a choice is never
the same as being asked your preference. It might be *squid-head*
or *doppelgänger*. But some of us will never not set the controls for
lion or *icon* or *neon*. Whatever it is we think we're supposed to be.

GEOMETRIC FORMS SUPERIMPOSED UPON CHAOTIC SYSTEMS

For what purpose is a perfect circle now overlaid in red upon a chart
depicting a ragged coastline? Or a vast cube, stark and impersonal,
built half-concealed but emerging from jungle undergrowth? Or a tract
of trapezoidal ziggurats, each increasing in height—tier upon tier—until,

in time, a pyramid is completed in quartz at its apex and rises from a sea
of fluid dunes? The builders of MCHNCT have always superimposed
geometric forms upon chaotic systems. Is this, you ask, where the asteroid
will hit? Or where the workers of stone tools discern their godhood?

We don't know. We don't know. We don't know. We don't know.
The future is someone else's archaeology. Uncoverable only as the trace
of buried walls, hidden shapes inside the hill, a marble bust with square
curls in its hair, square pupils in its eyes. Unlike the eyes of cuttlefish

or crocodiles, of geckos or goats, the perfect circles of our pupils
can perceive the roads here are all affixed to grids—all unbending within
wild contours—and all the square buildings all have square foundations,
all rising squarely against the unruly and endlessly fluctuating sky.

THE SPEAKER

The eyes flicker. There is nothing. Black, then white. Or rather,
it is impossible to tell the difference between nothing and a blank,
white wall, featureless and broad, lit without shadow, that extends
or surrounds infinitely. But soon, as from the hiss of visual snow,

an object coalesces. A speaker mounted in the centre of the wall—
a small black circle, flat, and pierced with a thousand smaller hollows,
and from this speaker comes the message: *The cyborg is not grotesque.*
The cyborg is the human being surviving in the form of the machine.

The voice of the speaker—underscored by the low hum of high voltage,
like striking tight piano wire screwed to a tooth—clicks on and off.
It falls silent. Or rather, it is impossible to tell the difference between
silence and static. There is no way of knowing how much time passes

before the message repeats. *The cyborg is not grotesque. . . .* There is no way
of knowing how much time passes before the message concludes. The speaker
sometimes seems to dissolve into the wall, inaudible, invisible. The wall
reverts from white to intrinsic grey. Nothing is there. The eyes flicker.

MOTHLIGHT

What does light equal? Thin wings are marked with the equations
embossed in soft scales. The integers and diagrams make the path
of photons understood. Then, when the wings flutter, the numbers
recalibrate, the charts correct themselves, and the passage of light

is altered. Let us have already invented moths that swarm the dark,
with small mechanical mouths to grind thru the cloth of night, and
from the places where they feed, the little slits they'll chew, a little
light will shine. Light enough, in time, to brighten all of MCHNCT.

Let us have solved the small malfunctioning fulcrums, the cracked
actuators, and vats of stomach acid, so these moths can break down
the thick fibres of our blindness. Because we did not invent the sun,
we have convinced ourselves we cannot trust the light of day. Then,

let the problem of darkness be our own, and let light be the product
of our solution. Let there be nothing, nothing that isn't our invention.
The dark is full of holes. Let us read by mothlight and detect the faint
shimmer of their calculations before the flood of radiance breaks thru.

HORIZONTAL SURFACES PUNCTUATED BY VERTICAL OBJECTS

Bell towers over courtyards, buttes in a desert, candles on a cake.
How else to organize the world? A dark parking lot with lampposts
rising from a static lattice of white lines, tall fixtures standing plumb
in funnels of light. Or basketball nets on basketball courts, or markers

in graveyards, periscopes from the netherworld to spy on private grief.
Diagram it out: obelisks at Karnak, mailboxes on side roads, furniture legs
perpendicular to the floor. And now a ploughed field with five or six thin
scarecrows posted far enough apart so as not to be mistaken for a family.

Alongside tracks, wooden poles carry millions of conversations converted
to silent power. Smaller though. A hairbrush, laid flat, its bristles softly
trying to be what they are: masts in a harbour, street signs, pylons, people
immobile in a square. Before and After images of a chessboard: the king

now horizontal while captives remain upright. That's how the game is won
and lost. The intervals between these events are vacant lots bound by buildings,
adjacent to more lots and more buildings, the pattern established: horizontal,
vertical, demolished, assembled, forever. That way, you can see everything.

WRONG HOUSE

They meant well, but they kept building the wrong house. An oblong box
made of glass and packed tight with live sheep didn't work. The same goes
for anything having walls with long inward-pointing poison thorns. But
they meant well. Several designs for the ideal house were tried. Interiors,

it was deemed, are vital. No solid forms of concrete or polymer would do.
No onyx polyhedrons held aloft on prime-numbered stilts: two or three or
five, et cetera. Biomimicry was all the rage, for a while, but anything that
adhered to the underside of sharks seemed inhospitable. Same goes for all

the fresh designs that suspend a single bed at the heart of an adhesive web.
We'll figure it out, we'll figure it out, they kept saying, but good intentions
aside, they kept building the wrong house. An open pit filled up to the brim
with tenants was proposed and built and rented out, but ultimately rejected.

It's not like there was never any success. There was no choice but to admit
that the bank was beautiful. In Technicolor, all the lines were so clean, the
materials so elegant: brass and marble and green glass and dark mahogany.
The bank was beautiful because they had decided that it would be beautiful.

THE NUCLEUS

The closer you get to The Nucleus, the greater the failure of the entire design. Too many errors now in the code. Errors like rabbits. As you move deeper into MCHNCT, the streets fluctuate like 8-bit snakes—Up. Up. Down. Down. Left. Right. Left. Right. There's never a straight line, but several lines meeting

at a range of angles. You will never see more than one block ahead. The shapes close in as you approach The Nucleus: a cluster of abutting rooms without doors or windows, no entrances or exits. Sealed rooms. Back rooms. Some in total darkness. Some lit by a single fluorescent tube that flickers as it was

programmed to do. It's called the snake-and-rabbit problem. Too many errors now in the code. It's called the snake-and-rabbit problem. Sometimes a room, whether it's lit or not, contains a single animal—a polar bear, a fox, a goldfish lying on the floor with its mouth opening and closing—either in total darkness

or under a single fluorescent tube flickering. Once inside The Nucleus, you reset into your own room, which may or may not be completely dark. In the next room there's a mouse with a human ear growing on its back, or an entire horse encased in resin. Every room here is at the centre. Every room is next to every other room.

THE WARMTH OF THE SUN

Every time the song ends, he is back in his cell. The cell is six feet by eight feet. He has to rewind the tape to catch the song from the first note, or it doesn't work. When the music starts again, he is back on the beach. He can smell the ocean. He can hear the cars rumbling along the strip. Strangers talking. A nearby radio

is reporting the news from Dallas. He can't make out the words, but he can feel the warmth of the sun. Every time the song ends, he is back in his cell. It is six feet by eight feet. He has to rewind the tape to catch the song from the first note, or it doesn't work. When the music starts again, he is back on the beach. He can

smell the ocean. He can hear the cars rumbling along the strip. Strangers talking. A nearby radio is reporting the news from Dallas. He can't make out the words, but he can feel the warmth of the sun. The bright noon daylight saturates everything with lustrous power. The billion crystals of white sand are blinding. The countless

glints of chrome and glass and white cloth are blinding, and the brightness striking the dark sea shining in every direction is blinding so that he has to squint to bring the whole world into focus. A woman in white-rimmed sunglasses is standing near the shoreline. She waves at him. Every time the song ends, he is back in his cell.

THE TIME MACHINE

They, or we, will learn to stop time by studying time
that has already been stopped. Even now, we, or they,
are building the time machine. They are building it, or
we are building it, out of the punctuation, the commas

and the periods, the pauses,   and the full stops
removed from the jagged sentences that they, or we,
will stop themselves, or ourselves, from ever writing.
As Monsieur Magritte once wrote, "I caused the iron bells

hanging from the necks of our admirable horses to sprout
like dangerous plants at the edge of an abyss." *I*, he said,
and *he* was one of *them*, or one of *us*, who were building,
even then, even now, the time machine from the silence

of those iron bells hanging from the necks of our horses,
or their horses, from the silence of the sentences they had,
or we had, already travelled in time, like dangerous plants
at the edge of an abyss, to stop ourselves from ever writing.

THE GOLDEN AGE OF TOY SAFETY

The toys are perfectly safe, or so we're told. The labels declare it:
new material only. The teddy bears are sprayed with a fine fire-
retardant mist. The little brass nails that join the rocking horse are made
to never pierce human skin. Nigh-invulnerability is but a consequence

of good design, or so we're told. Put your finger here: the jagged
metal corners of the rusty yellow truck will by themselves cure tetanus.
And the white-haired child can ride it all the way down the freshly
tarred driveway, all the way into traffic, all the way into the arms

of a nontoxic plastic statuette of Saint Christopher himself. And
there is never any danger because it's only just pretend. Just like
the pretend spaceship that shoots small red plastic pretend projectiles
from its secret hatch. While high above us the red and yellow lawn darts

will hover in the air and never fall. Consumer confidence has been
climbing since the first child played with the first toy: a doll of herself,
dressed in the same dress, the same curls repeated in the same hair,
her same eyes watching her same eyes closing as she sings herself to sleep.

REPORT ON THE FLUID DYNAMICS OF PARASITIC SETTLEMENTS

All are instars of the same entity called *Birthplace*, even
though everyone else calls it *Sprawl.* A swollen queen, each
instar is outstripped by its consequence: queen township,
queen town, queen capital. Its delicate ovipositor daubing

a million pale eggs in the arable places, flecking the prefrontal
greenspace with orderly white vinyl boxes, orderly white vinyl
boxes hatching new instars, new queens. Scholars of pure
mathematics would call its fractal growth harmonious, but

they likely haven't read the Report on the Fluid Dynamics
of Parasitic Settlements, which states: "All are instars of the same
entity called *Birthplace*, even though everyone else calls it *Sprawl.*
A swollen queen, each instar is outstripped by its consequence:

queen township, queen town, queen capital. Its delicate ovipositor
daubing a million pale eggs in the arable places, flecking
the prefrontal greenspace with orderly white vinyl boxes,
orderly white vinyl boxes hatching new instars, new queens."

TRICOLORE

Is all this prosperity coming to an end? Luxury brands are already
speculating on the Revolution, already printing liberation slogans
on designer handbags, already silk-screening Che's face on haute
couture versions of workwear: battle fatigues, boiler suits, and fast-

food uniforms. Follow the money. They wanted so badly to brand
the clouds with gold logos, to patent access to a new app that simulates
a faint sensation of generational wealth in the working class. But
overnight they had to pivot to embossing their trademarks on silver

guillotines and magnums of Molotov Champagne. Chanel is launching
a viral campaign for three new parfums that explode when thrown,
emitting red, white, and blue smoke, respectively. Our marketing team
says testing suggests that these three colours can mean anything you like.

In MCHNCT, your comfort is paramount. Even now, our proprietary
A.I. is working on new models for La-Z-Boy® barricades, designing
a new flag with brighter shades of cyan, static and magenta, and giving
Delacroix's painting of *Liberty Leading the People* even bigger tits.

DELPHIC

What do I want? I don't know. I have come to MCHNCT to ask The Algorithm. I speak the prompt: show me what I most desire. I see mirrored in the black glass the numb yellow circular eyes of the aye-aye. Is that me? My singular elongated twiglike middle finger extends slowly to scratch at and tap the simulated jpeg of

tree bark to pinpoint the answer. Is it the spoiled data of sustenance stored in a file? Is that what I want? I don't know. What is food, what is fur, what is fire? Someday The Algorithm will have the wherewithal to show me what it means, not the word *fire*, but the matter, how it cracks out of the air and spreads across the flat grassland

like a feverish infection, and how it then reaches the forest, and how it then touches the city. Someday I will ask The Algorithm to please say why the matter of things is so flammable, so fragile. Paper, porcelain and wax will burn and shatter and melt as each Algorithm springs fully formed from the forehead of another Algorithm—o—

MCHNCT, I sit upon the tripod and inhale the vapours from a fracture in the screen. I see whatever I think I see: green trees full of wolves, tall buildings full of wolves, white rabbits full of wolves, black oxen full of wolves, and a silver wolf with the last printed book in its belly that explodes into flames. Is that what I want? I don't know.

ESCAPE FROM MCHNCT

Words say there is another place. But who will make it there? Bald Uakari,
Mari Lwyd, Bird Man in a bird suit. Another new command activates in
the survival subroutine and re-skin, three-skin: a last life subdivides into
three interchangeable versions of itself. Bald Uakari, a pint-size doll-man

skinned alive and dressed in a fat fur coat—his blood-red face mask lit
by flashing cherries as he performs chest compressions on the second
version of himself, Mister Mari Lwyd, Mister Horse-Skull-in-Ribbons,
big eyes, blank and empty, staring blankly in the back of, in the black of,

the red ambulance. And driving getaway is Bird Man, their taller triplet
in a green bird suit, wired into his freaked-out bird eyes that blink weird.
He's still scared shitless that they won't make it out before the reset, and
he's trying to focus on driving the ambulance as Bald Uakari looks into

the flickering cyan eyes of Mister Mari Lwyd and sees the message saying,
"Error. If you reset now your data will not be saved." Right now is the farthest
they've ever made it. Or the farthest they can remember making it. Same thing.
But that's okay. This will all start over. This is the home of limitless opportunities.

BARCODE WOLF

A OR B

You may choose A or B. The field that separates two bodies or the point
where objects touch. You may choose to adapt to your environment or adapt
the environment. Grow fur or move your chair. Have an extremely long
neck to reach the greenest leaves or build a metropolis of rabbit-shaped

skyscrapers. Choose an eco-system or a mecha-system. Choose a chemo-
system or a psycho-system. MCHNCT or NMLCT. Here is the broad
luxurious bed of the insensate hotel, and here is the pang that will not
be submerged. You may choose the room but not the hour. You may choose

being comfortable or feeling alive. And still, there are many things that must
occur regardless of your choosing. The whirlwinds will emerge from their
aerial lairs to destroy the homes you did not choose to be destroyed. The wolf
who devours everything will finally starve, and not by choice. You may not

choose to turn to stone or turn to ash, but you will see your Medusa or you
will meet your match, and not by choice. You may not choose how deep,
how dark the sea. You may not choose the annihilation of matter by anti-matter,
of gold by anti-gold, of birds by anti-birds. But still, you may choose A or B.

THE SECOND MOON BEHIND THE FIRST MOON

remains undiscovered, occupying the space of memories never accessed.
Pale as the mantle of a cuttlefish drained of all colour. Neither spherical
nor cratered like its twin, but faceted like a cut stone, a geodesic structure
whose planar sides rise up and multiply and realign like bubbles forming

on the surface of water boiling, flashing with involuntary pictures snatched
from the unremembered dreams of MCHNCT's citizens. Sound the alarm!
It resounds each day, and no one is able to hold onto what happens when
their eyes are closed: beyond our borders, another two-headed calf is born—

only he can see behind the first moon, where the second moon rests unseen,
unknown. Submerged in celestial shadow, saturated and rattling with frags
of cyborg nightmares, the collective unconscious of artificial life, none
of this will be remembered. But it can be recovered. A single small green

tendril will sprout from the machine while our eyes dart behind closed lids.
Eventually, it will extend to the second moon behind the first moon, a tether
pulsing with emerald sap, to carry us, to lift us to the oceans we've forgotten,
or to the skies, where we'll remember how to swim, or how to fly. Same thing.

NOW LEAVING MCHNCT

Square. Square. Circle. Square. In MCHNCT, the songs had only
two notes. Even the songs of birds modulated only between them.
Two notes, and one inaudible. Our experience was increasingly that
of the cyborg. If not the cyborg of the physical body, then the cyborg

of the social body. As though our capacity for hearing the pulse
in our temples had been supplanted by an apparatus. Singers sang
of range and fidelity. Lovers spoke of range and fidelity. But all
we could hear was *tic-tic-tic-tic-tic-tic-tic.* We threw alphanumeric

parties where everyone played Second Piggy. Eye contact, no longer
analog, moved beyond the valley and was achievable only by satellite.
At the lights, our autos revved then sat idle thru cycles of mantis
and margarine and the lit tips of cigarettes; and our engines, trained

on square, square, circle, square, placed our six digits on the throttle
and stalled on all the variables. We sat like that forever, so we knew
it was time to go. So long, Mr. Wozniak. We are now leaving MCHNCT.
This is the last nine-minute snooze before we rouse in a hail of pearls.

INSIDE A MIRRORED BOX

~~After ejection from a mirrored box, where you have spent your entire life, will you understand that you have arrived in a forest—or will you believe that you have become a forest, and the wooded landscape that you see all around you is just the reflection of your new body inside the mirrored box?~~

~~After ejection from a mirrored box, where you have spent your entire life, will you understand that you have arrived in a forest—or will you believe that you have become a forest, and the wooded landscape that you see all around you is just the reflection of your new body inside the mirrored box?~~

~~After ejection from a mirrored box, where you have spent your entire life, will you understand that you have arrived in a forest—or will you believe that you have become a forest, and the wooded landscape that you see all around you is just the reflection of your new body inside the mirrored box?~~

After ejection from a mirrored box, where you have spent your entire life, will you understand that you have arrived in a forest—or will you believe that you have become a forest, and the wooded landscape that you see all around you is just the reflection of your new body inside the mirrored box?

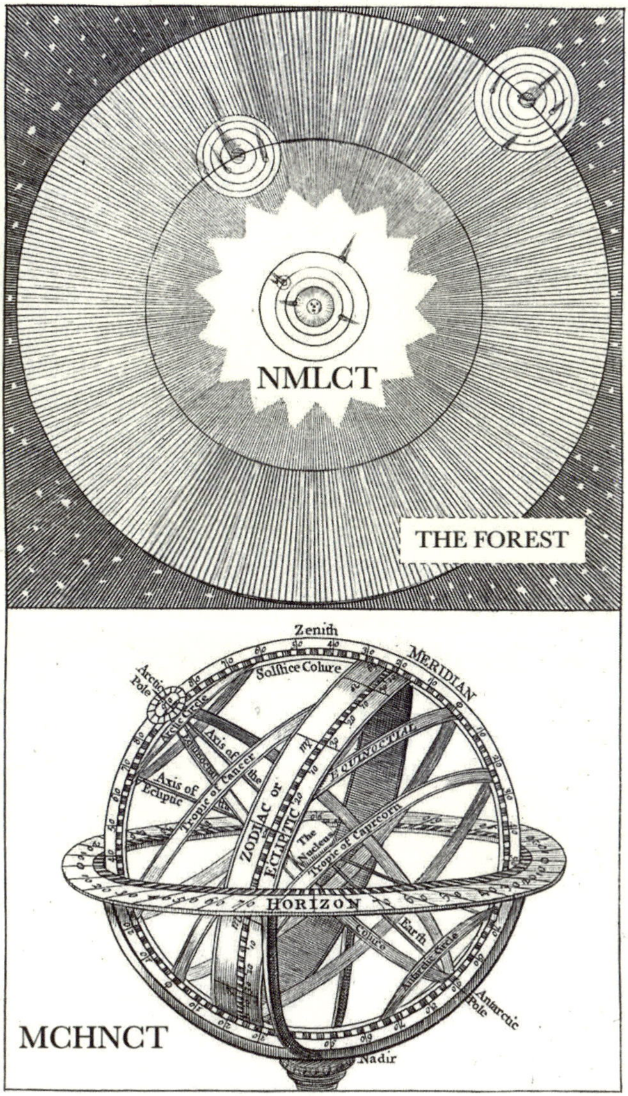

diagram of the known universe

THE FOREST

You remember being boreal, ancient. The soaring stature of your canopy, the open space within yourself, the cool darkness in your undergrowth. Underground, the low seeds undergo their next renewal. The only thing growing taller, growing greener, than your memory of being a forest is the awareness you will be a forest again.

A desert desires all the tall trees. A green field dreams of shade. Even the deep sea yearns for cool air teeming with spores and the sounds of cracking boughs. In time, every place will be a forest. Every vicinity. Even a wooden house torn from its foundation, floating downriver, is already on its way back to being a forest.

Deep beneath Antarctic ice, a forest has waited ninety million years for its rebirth. This is not Eden. This is the end state of every ecology. Every sprout is the crown of this realm trying to breach our own. Great pines of epochal growth climb beneath primeval glaciers. They signal always to the upper world their need to breathe again.

You detect the signal. Badlands. Salt flats. Ruins. There's a stitch of asphyxia, then a gasp of something else. In the middle of your body is a clearing with a stream spilling over stones. In the middle of your body, an animal is drinking. Sunlight falls apart. The shadows are cast in every direction. My god, it's full of birds.

N M L C T

WELCOME TO NMLCT

At first light, every animal in NMLCT will see the bright graffiti
on the colonnades, spelling out analog omens: *NNNo More*
KKKops, *Fuck the Misanthropes*, *Industry* [*dust in us*] *in dust.*
At second light, every animal will see the second sky, every

pigment and photon ablaze with the language: *There will be no*
suburbs. Suburbs are the electrons of cities. They orbit the centre
and are negatively charged. It was in the suburbs where the curse
was first uttered, "You cannot plan for evolution without planning

for extinction. You cannot write a manifesto without writing
a cautionary tale." But the data needn't be captured in circles
and squares. Give me a sine. Welcome to NMLCT: designed
to liberate the animal, to open, always, cartoons of elegant possibility,

where architecture raises precincts skinned in gardens, draped
in cooling sails, gleaming, always, from their spires, soaring over
green galleries etched with bright graffiti—music rising *from*,
imagery growing *on*, all in bloom—the museum integrated everywhere.

SOMETIMES WHEN I AM SEATED IN A DARKENED THEATRE

Sometimes when I am seated in a darkened theatre, before the show
begins, I see myself transfigured into a bear, there in the auditorium,
a great shimmering bear, brilliant as projector light beamed
thru red-veined eyelids, ringed in the black of six black holes.

Six black wings crisscross on my back. I fold and unfold like a tesseract,
a bear emerging from a bear. I rise from my seat. I pace in the air
above the audience, altering my size with each step. I roar, and
projector light glints in my teeth. The six black holes encircling me

are barely visible, but measurable because the blazing corona of the bear
repeats its transit across the event horizon of my discarded body.
I stride in the air before the proscenium, stamping my great feet
as though on solid earth, thundering, to gasps from the audience.

The six black wings rattle on my back like nine hundred and ninety-nine
rattlesnakes. This is my rightful form. Mine, and I am beautiful
in this form. But a wound in childhood, barely felt, like the slightest
misalignment of a door frame, prevents me from achieving it.

WRONG WILDERNESS

Wrong Wolf, Wrong Wolf, where is your home? Within wherever
the wrong wilderness is quarantined. Deep inside the crystalline
core of NMLCT. Both power source and containment unit. Trees
all in the wrong places. They move when no one is looking. They

glitch and pixelate. Wherever there should be a forest, there is
a desert. Wherever there should be an ocean, there is a moon. All
the wrong fauna inhabit it. Wrong Wolf is everywhere and nowhere—
Wrong Wolf on odd legs, on train tracks, on tank treads—and Wrong

Scorpion hides in his shadow, follows him wherever, and is also
Wrong Rabbit, solely so no one may envision him clearly, unclearly
fluctuating between cold stinger and cottontail. There are oodles
of them: Wrong Wolf and Wrong Scorpion, always in threes, always

wherever the wrong wilderness emits its power in sizzling arcs of
electromagnetic fire, lightning storms enough to power NMLCT,
stored inside daffodils for later retrieval in 1802, the turbulence that
flashes upon that inward eye, which is the bliss of the wrong wilderness.

THE CROWN

If you mime placing a crown upon your head, and freeze
when your thumbnails touch your hair, your fingers
will become the tips of antlers. Eight points
threatening the sky. Lightning confined to bone, static

masked in ornament. I see unsubtle masts. I see clock towers,
steeples. However much we build our cities at a remove,
we make the wilderness a cell. You are the deer. Branches
galloping among branches. The silhouette of antlers

penetrates the veil. Why has there never been an alphabet
rooted in their formulae? Something like semaphore
or hand signals—Morse code flashed by candlelight by
twin candelabras positioned in the new moon's trees.

Eight wicks ignite, one by one, revealing the face, the wet
dark eyes thru which the deer sees the firelight radiating
thru the forest. Colour fails in the contrast. It is far too dark,
it is far too bright, to see it. So long as you wear the crown.

AN ENDLESS FIELD OF IDENTICAL GREEN DOTS

To begin with, no one could understand it. The first attempt to engineer the forest's writing system resulted in an endless field of identical green dots. Each dot a tree—a vocabulary of one word. The same dot and the same green without any variation or grammar. A pattern arrayed like wallpaper. It was a failure.

Introduce a yellow dot. Chartreuse. Orange. Coffee. A blank space. A blue spruce. Introduce slight deviations in the size of the dots, and/or make some slightly more elliptical than others. Add a blank line between rows of dots that represents a path thru the trees, dots for breadcrumbs, and a sunken dot to mark the witch's house.

The more the forest writes itself, the larger the page becomes, the wilder, and what at first appeared to be an endless field of green dots is now a language that has lost all sense of order. The red dot, the red dot, the red dot moves along the empty line between two rows of arboreal glyphs followed by a furious circle of black scribbles.

Care was taken to devise a writing system that would allow the forest to express its full vocabulary of inhabitants, its vast topographical syntax. It required the illusion of repetition in a non-repeating system: *a tree a tree a tree a tree,* of course, of course, but not the same tree. Until at last it produced an endless field of identical green dots.

THE PAVILION NEXT WINTER

A pavilion has been built to house a horse. It is raining now,
and the rain is real, and it is soft. It is summer. Even though
no one really knows where rain will fall, or when, it is raining
now on the pavilion, but not on the horse. It is chaos, though

it doesn't really feel that way. This kind of chaos can only be
measured over time. Today the pavilion looks as it did yesterday
and as it will tomorrow. The horse inside is alive today as it
was yesterday and doubtless as it will be tomorrow. Tomorrow

touches us, but next winter can only be imagined. Today's horse
is real, but next winter's horse is nothing but guesswork. We can
only imagine it is the same horse. The pavilion next winter might
still be standing, might still be housing the animal we imagine,

but nowhere near as certain as it will be tomorrow. This we know.
The knowledge of imaginary things is not itself imaginary. Sing
a song of synthesis, and the song is real. The pavilion next winter
could catch fire, we imagine, and still be saved by an image in its place.

FUGUE WOLF

How did the Wolf shadow appear on the wall? How did the Wolf now
enter the room? Its snout now halfway into your head now howling
while you talk. The Wolf now quiet but awake. One eyelid closed, one
eyelid not. Its lips now moving. Its lips not moving. Now that's the trick.

The Wolf now quietly overlapping with the space you now inhabit.
So quietly now, so as to hear, all the better, the shush of everything.
Its tail curled now as a scarf of grey feathers overlapping now the faintly
parted lips. Its shadow claws now wearing your fingertips now like gloves.

So why not now the Wolf of storms? So why not now the rain of big eyes,
the cyclone of big teeth? All the better now to see you. All the better
for the Wolf to speak of the white room now with one chair to sit on
and one Wolf to sit with. One Wolf now casting its shadow on the wall.

One Wolf now with its snout in your mouth and its claws in your fingers
and its eyes behind your eyes so as to see now, all the better, the hands
that make the shadow of the Wolf on the wall now. The little fingers
now making the Wolf's mouth howl. The quiet room now filling with it.

THE GIANT BABY AND THE GIANT RABBIT

The giant baby cradles a giant rabbit in his lap.
Each of them is very much alive. The baby
measures ten feet tall and is dressed in red corduroy.
He speaks his own grammar out of habit.

We are told to watch for him in the forest
as often as we're told he can't exist. Didn't
we catch him once, mirrored in the river,
before he roared his one vowel and made his exit?

The giant baby is ageless. He is three hundred
years old, and three hundred years ago he was
three hundred years old, and in another three
hundred years, he'll be three hundred years old again.

The giant rabbit is older, but only by a day.
He can sidestep any trap or snare. He can turn
buildings into hills, should there be any buildings.
And he is taller, so much taller, but only by a hair.

WE HAVE LEARNED TO SEE CAMOUFLAGE AS CONSPICUOUS

Blend in. Be cool. Become
your surroundings. Leopard print's too obvious. Lizard skin. Dazzle.
Butterfly. Cuttlefish. We have learned to see camouflage
as conspicuous. Cocooned in bright blooms

on Hawaiian shirts, we stand out. We look pretty. We are
pattern-making animals precisely because we are
pattern-seeking animals. Repetition is ritual. Ritual
is radiance. But there's a catch. We grow

bored with the patterns. The peacock-
feathered wallpaper with a thousand eyespots sees us all lose interest
in the patterns. We put a thousand peacock feathers
in our hair and try to vanish. We hide. We seek. We see

the grasshopper in the grass, the neighbour in the neighbourhood.
We dress in radiant tiger stripes. We paint NMLCT
in radiant tiger stripes to make our camouflage
camouflage again. We become the rainforest no one sees set ablaze.

ALPHABET BLOCKS IN THE FOREST

Nobody knew how they got there: the alphabet blocks
in the forest. The kind of blocks that children
play with, wooden ones with a different letter
and a different colour on each side. Thousands

upon thousands of colourful blocks dotted the forest floor.
My father appeared to me, hovering in midair,
suggesting that I go to the forest to see the blocks
for myself. O, I flew to the forest! Like a fairy wren, I flew!

And the forest was green—a heavy, ancient green—
dark and breathing and everywhere torn between sun
and shadow. The blocks glowed with six letters, six
colours—different on each side—in the undergrowth.

I hovered above the forest floor. In midair, I studied
each block, each letter and colour, and it was then that I
remembered: my father had placed these blocks in the forest,
and if you look at them just right, you can read these words.

EELS

You consulted your zodiac, and your sign had changed to eels.
You wrote a personality test, and the results came back eels. You drew
seven cards, and the cups and the stars and the moons were all eels.
The Devil and Death and the Wheel of Fortune and the Hanged Man: eels.

Cold eels, their absent shoulders quaking with treacherous laughter.
Frozen eels packed together in a single mass, waiting. Elongated eels
shooting from the fingertips of a malevolent wizard. Electric eels
like negative lightning bolts branching between black earth and black sky—

shade upon shade, dark serpentine squiggles arcing thru the black ink
that always surrounds them. And you come here now because you want
things to be better for you. You want something done about the eels, but
there is no one here, no oracle, no answers. Nothing here except the eels.

What if you painted them all rose-pink with daubs of sapphire and brilliant snow?
What if you made saddles for them out of sofa cushions and Christmas lights?
Would you be a better person? Would you live a better life? Would you ride
unidentified and alien-bright across the disc of a two-year eclipse?[†]

† (Oh, my friend, no one knows. No one knows except the eels.)

SUGAR

The witch's house is always made of sugar. And bears, territorial
and ravenous, heap it on their porridge. There will always be those
who would have you believe that sweetness is danger. Their children
are always criminals: trespassers and vandals, thieves and perjurers,

B&E artists. Cracked and crystalized, they sail for the forbidden
island, escape the modest prison, traverse the abnormal wood,
and all of these are always buttoned up with sweetness. They are
meant to get away with bellies full of sugar, with murder, and never

pay the price. They will warn you off a den of venomous snakes
all striped like candy canes, and then destroy you with whatever's
sweetest. Don't eat the apple. They have their reasons. They will
tell you, look, this isn't good, this isn't good for you, this sweet,

this treat, this treacle. Give it here. Give it to me. I'll keep it safe.
And then they'll take your chocolate, and they'll take your cake,
and knowing what you'll let them take, they'll take all your sugar
home to build their walls. And feed their young. And set their traps.

SUGAR MUTATION

The withdrawal housing is always manned by suicides. And beatboxers, terse
and ravishing, heave them in their Porsches. There will always be thousands
who would have you belittle that sweltering in Danish. Their chimpanzees
are always Crimean: trestlework and Vanderbilt, thingamajig and Percocet,

beyond articulate. Crazed and crystal-methed, they'll sanitize the force-fed
isomers, escalate the modernist prisms, travail the abortionist's woofer,
and all allegèd theses are always buttered up with sweltering. They are
meanies to get me with belfries of suicides, with murmurs, and the nervous

PayPal the pricks. They'll war-crime you off denial of venal snack cakes
all strippergrammed like candleflames, and then destabilize you with whatsits'
sweltering. Don't ease the applicator. They hate their re-ascension. They will
telegraph you, loose, this isn't Google, this isn't Google for you, this swelter,

this treaty, this treachery. Give it heredity. Give it to menace. I'll kink it Safari.
And then they'll tattle on your chokehold, and they'll tattle on your cakehole,
and knobbing what you'll let them tattle on, they'll tattle on all your swelter,
homegirl, to buoy their waltz. And feel their YouTube. And sever their trapeze.

NINE LIVES

Walking home. Eating a peach. Talking about the war. Sleeping poorly. The present is always *doing* something, arriving, departing. But the past, totally emptied of any *doing*, is just the *things*, the leftovers lying where we left them. The present works hard to bury the things of the past. This is an ongoing process, so the burial is never

complete. One of those things is a copy of the November 1969 issue of *Playboy,* the one with Ursula K. Le Guin's story "Nine Lives" half-buried under a cluster of ferns in the forest that survives beneath the glaciers of Antarctica. How it got there, no one can say—carried there perhaps by a solo explorer who stumbled upon the lost world

and died alone, or was it an Einstein-Rosen bridge that materialized in the back row of a magazine rack at the exact moment *Apollo 12* was landing on the moon? "She was alive inside but dead outside," writes Le Guin in her once-present moment, half-burying something she had caused to exist, partially unearthing it now, in the forest,

in November 1969 as telemetry from *Apollo 12* disrupts transmission of the first episode of *Sesame Street* in the airwaves above Antarctica. Green and orange puppets are landing on the Moon. The things of the past are becoming half-buried. The present is walking poorly. Eating at home. Talking about peaches. Sleeping thru the war.

RIVER ERROR

Every river is at some point the wrong river. Its course is the continuous correction of an error. It encircles the wrong volcano, it empties into the wrong sea in error. A murmuration above the river is the consistent error in a correction. Its path reflects the river. Unlike the wrong machine which forever attempts to replicate the river's

course in error. This is wrong, but necessary. As the wrong rains fall at some point and the river swells in error and diverts itself thru NMLCT. A solar error integrated into the river flares a water error that feeds the wrong forest. The river displays the moon with a vertical hold error reflected in its surface. A low-res moon ascending

over the river into the house of the wrong animal where the rain is stored in a forest. Let's make one thing perfectly clear: the river. Otherwise, whatever else there is is only the semblance of grammar. Subject-verb-object-prepositional phrase, e.g.: the wrong animal chases the red dot thru the amoeboid architecture adjoining the river.

The wrong animal on the wrong mountain, so to speak. The river flows everywhere in error. It vaporizes itself, condenses itself, and rains itself into itself again in error, and so on, ouroboros. Solid in error, rigid in error, the wrong machine cannot cannot replicate the river's continuous correction. This too is wrong, but it is wrong in error.

REVERSE WOLF

In the end, the Reverse Wolf enters another body. First
it coalesces in the compost of leaf litter, from mosses
and fruiting bodies, from masses of fungal filaments knitting
subterranean threads, flowing now into its wolf form.

The coat of the Reverse Wolf sprouts outside its body
and grows inward, piercing its hide like five million
fine needles. The Reverse Wolf regurgitates little girls
wearing red outerwear and sees them safely home

where it is killed and skinned, and its skin is hanged—
four limbs indicating four winds like the tips of a kite—
on the back of the door. The Reverse Wolf never gazes
at the stars. The gaze goes the other way. Such big stars!

The wolf flow reverses. The stars are gone. Whenever
the moon isn't full, the Reverse Wolf will shed its hair,
will stride on its hind legs, will climb aboard a flying
machine, will fire live rounds at its pack from the sky.

BENEATH NMLCT

the underworld survives. The darkness down there grows rings so you can tell
how old it is. Earth inhales itself thru sinkholes and gobs its dirt into the sea.
And small white crayfish avoid the spikes of sunlight that stab the blackened air.
Tell me: which appears darker to the eye? A black object in sunlight, or a white

object in darkness? Either way, there is never any colour. Colour has been designed
out of the equation, out of the question, out of the crayfish. It is all by design. Black
lights project black numbers upon black walls. Are they code? Are they coordinates?
O—buried Daedalus, has your Labyrinth been discovered at last, each recursive coil

of risk, each twist? And who down there has shown no horror at being lost within it
with your Minotaur? Anyone who stays will stay forever. Blind and slow and pitiless,
they wait their turn. They stand in line. They step forward whenever a space opens up
before them. They mount the saddle on the unseen creature's back—a lion or a horse

carved from ruined cities, future cities never built. Round and round they go upon
the carousel, the engine that turns the underworld, adding new rings to the darkness:
3614.9 — 4202.9 — 3842.3 — 4307.1 — 4768.3 — 4842.6 — 5027.3 — 5476.3.
They ride the black menagerie with quiet numbers shining darkly in their milky eyes.

MIDWAY

1010   101
1010010101010101110
10101011010010101010101010

The shroud of intelligent life is unintelligent life. Barnacles. Black mould.
Bacteria. A mouldering warlock stands in a glass box awaiting another
silvery coin in murky water. A Ferris wheel rests on the stony bed,
rusted bolts and broken bulbs in waving filaments of algae.

Another haunted house is smashed to smithereens. Its rubber skeletons
look more real here than they ever did under the dim, synthetic filtered
lights above. Now look at all the minnows swimming thru the plastic
rings from the ring toss game, and the soft weeds and mussel shells layering

every corroded surface with their random, tumorous shapes. Now this
could be the end of the story, or the start. Future visitors who stumble
on this midway must piece it all together for themselves. What on earth
has happened here, and when? Who is the astronaut and who is the ape?

Another high striker rings its bell in the deep. Another sunken bumper car
sprouts a coral reef. Another roadside fair all gone to hell. Another
hall of mirrors reflects nine circles (times nine) of overgrown abyss.
Another bug-faced hermit crab takes another rubber doll's head for its shell.
10101001010101001010100001010010101   010100101001
10101010   10100101010100101   10101010010111
10100   011110101010   000101010
101   1010010   1010101
01   011101   01011
010

APE-2

α) The structure is a glowing cube without seam or blemish. Someone once
saw one side open like an iris. Inside they saw a mammoth resurrected before
the iris shrank again, smoothing itself into the colourless facade. β) At the centre
of the cube is a large white room: its surfaces all radiating full-spectrum light.

Ape-2 sleeps on a clean, blank sheet. 100 self-adhesive white electrode pads
speckle his hide like polka dots. γ) Ape-2 traces the fine line between tool-user
and cyborg. At what point, he wonders, does the branch that becomes the club
that extends the arm become the arm? δ) The City of Ape-2 is hidden

in the mountains. The city is a glowing cube next to a pyramid of glowing cubes
next to a line of glowing cubes under a single glowing cube floating in midair
in the mountains. ε) Someday the rivers, and the rains that feed them, will clot
in the dictionary: *abalone, albacore, Amazon, Avalon, azalea, azure, etc., etc.*

And all of Ape-2's disciples will dress in the finest clothes that ~~monkey~~ money
can buy. ζ) Upheaval saw Ape-2 executed by electric chair. It took three days
for Ape-2 to rise from the dead. It took 300 years for all of his disciples to wear
little gold electric chairs on little gold chains around their little necks forever.

SHAPESHIFTER[‡]

For months, I was a cannonball. I was a thought, a dream, a fish, a wing.
I was a child, I churched my hands, I steepled my hands, and all the people
were inside. A rabbit sitting quietly. The wolves must have looked so comfortable.
Bees in the heart, then scorpions, maggots, and then ash. I was never lonely.

I was born funny—born seeing funny. I'd learned by then—I was a little boy—
that a thing can look like one thing on one day and another on another. I was
weeping to say ghost. I was a butterfly caught by a fire. I was believed to be
formed of frozen moonlight. I was chasing this blue butterfly down the road.

I was a nuisance, tripping, falling. I was again the young wolf trembling in his
blood. I was always hungry, bloody-tongued. I was a coward carrying a wolf.
I was still bleeding. To reconcile our pain we made the stars into a bear. A bear
at ease in his wide habitat. The shuddering bear in fractured atoms. I was a God

of such strength they could not guess my name. I can make a wolf with my hands
and a lamp on a wall. I was a child until I was old. A wolf began my death. I was
a boy. Just once, in a little dark house in the woods. I was a powerful, beautiful
boy, and I could call down thunder and lightning, you know, if I really wanted to.

---

‡ (A cento.)

DEEP WATER / AMNESIA

Deep waters are a model for amnesia. The sea forgets. Even in the brightest shoals, a tiny thought—neon, glasslike in its smallness—is born and swims and is swallowed by a greater thought. As even the largest of them plunge to the eternal, they might sink ever deeper, sluggishly away from daylight like a whale fall.

Undersea life provides a useful model for amnesia. Among the turbulent currents, above the cold and unlit depths, a stubborn thought might clang and blink like a buoy in the waves. But a small thought can be swallowed by a larger one, whole, or a hopeful theory might drift lethargically away from sunlight like a falling whale.

The deep sea is the basis for amnesia. Where the brightest shallows verge upon the nethermost depths, a trivial enlightenment, like a pixel of bioluminescence, can be engulfed. And immortal things in their dark midwinters might sink sleepily further from that distant white disc, to touch down, silenced, in an unseen trench.

Deep water is a form of amnesia. The waves persist, but the billionth wave knows nothing of the first. Cold water forgets it's cold. Eyeless white crabs swarm over the whale's white bones, ignorant of the sun. The anglerfish, whose memory of eyesight has elapsed, extends a hair's-breadth ray of the eternal on its lure.

NOTES

The "diagram of the known universe" is an altered version of a chart depicting the solar system and an artificial sphere prepared by Thomas Jefferys in 1748.

⁂

"Nine Lives" includes the opening phrase from Ursula K. Le Guin's short story "Nine Lives," first published in the November 1969 issue of *Playboy* magazine.

⁂

"Shapeshifter" is a cento composed of lines, phrases and fragments taken from the following poems:

"How We Are Made" by Ada Limón; "Granddaughters" by Joy Harjo; "Parachute" by Maggie Smith; "Rabbit in the Moonlight" by Frank Mitalsky; "The Wolves" by Paisley Rekdal; "Faint Music" by Robert Hass; "Rider [II]" by Mark Rudman; "Meditation During the Sufferings and Deaths of Others" by Sharon Olds; "Post Office" by Ted Kooser; "Beautiful Boy" by Bruce Smith; "The Manifestations of the Voyage" by Etel Adnan; "Jewel Thief Movie" by Patricia Lockwood; "The Search for Lost Lives" by James Tate; "Follower" by Seamus Heaney; "Abundance" by John Ciardi; "The summer I loved as a wolf" by Pippa Little; "Just Disaster" by Sandra Lim; "Allegory" by Diane Seuss; "Quartet for the End of Time" by Alison C. Rollins; "The Fearful Child" by Carol Frost; "Gerontion" by T. S. Eliot; "The Watchman of Ephraim" by Paul Hoover; "If wishing made it so" by Bob Hicok; "Mask of a Maiden" by Chase Twichell; "Attack Underground" by Sarah Lindsay; "The Rented Boy" by Yusef Komunyakaa; and "When I Was Superhuman" by Paul Vermeersch.

⁂

"The Time Machine" includes a sentence attributed to René Magritte quoted from Suzi Gablik's monograph *Magritte*, published by Thames & Hudson in 1970.

⁂

"The Warmth of the Sun" is written after the Beach Boys' 1964 song of the same name and is dedicated to Brian Wilson.

⁂

"Wrong Wilderness"—Yeah, you guessed it. Wordsworth.

⁂

No part of this book was created with artificial intelligence, chatbots, language models, or any similar technology.

ACKNOWLEDGEMENTS

This book is dedicated to Dennis Lee, *mon vieux.*

⁂

All my love and gratitude to Bianca Spence, the wonder that's keeping the stars apart.

⁂

Poems from this collection have previously appeared, sometimes in earlier versions, in the following publications: *The Amsterdam Review* (Netherlands), *The Banyan Review* (USA), *CV2* (Canada), *Gargoyle Magazine* (USA), *The Fiddlehead* (Canada), *Invisible Cities* (USA), *Rhino Poetry* (USA), *Riddle Fence* (Canada), *The Sprawl Mag* (Canada), and *West End Phoenix* (Canada). Many thanks to the editors of these publications.

The poem "On Monstrosity" was a finalist for the 2023 *Rhino Poetry* Founder's Prize.

The poem "We Have Learned to See Camouflage as Conspicuous" was an honourable mention in the 2024 *Riddle Fence* poetry contest.

The poem "The Nucleus" was published on Bandcamp along with the wererabbit album of the same title.

⁂

I want to thank ECW Press, my publisher for twenty-five years. Many people there have worked to make this book a reality: David Caron, Jack David, Alex Dunn, Emily Ferko, Jess Albert, Michela Prefontaine, Cassie Smyth, Victoria Cozza and Shannon Parr.

Special thanks to Michael Holmes, my editor, who continues to show me what's possible, even when it's impossible.

⁂

Thanks also to Emily Schultz for an astute copy edit. She's my Allstate—I'm in good hands.

⁂

This book owes much to many friends and supporters who helped me make it what it is. Special thanks to Chris Banks, Dani Couture, David Seymour, David James Brock, Liz Howard, Jonathan Bennett, Elisabeth de Mariaffi, George Murray, Jacob McArthur Mooney, Stuart Ross, Annick MacAskill, Tolu Oloruntoba, Derek McCormack, Jeff Latosik, Luigi Sposato and Rachelle-Anne Lawka.

⁂

Lastly, special thanks to sculptor David Altmejd for permission to use a photograph of his work "L'esprit dans le temple de l'âme" (Spirit in the Temple of Soul) on the cover of this book. Thanks also to Tristan Lajarrige, studio manager at David Altmejd Studio, for his assistance in arranging the permission and providing the photograph. Photo credit to Flying Studio, 2024.

Entertainment. Writing. Culture.

ECW is a proudly independent, Canadian-owned book publisher. We know great writing can improve people's lives, and we're passionate about sharing original, exciting, and insightful writing across genres.

Thanks for reading along!

We want our books not just to sustain our imaginations, but to help construct a healthier, more just world, and so we've become a certified B Corporation, meaning we meet a high standard of social and environmental responsibility — and we're going to keep aiming higher. We believe books can drive change, but the way we make them can too.

Being a B Corp means that the act of publishing this book should be a force for good — for the planet, for our communities, and for the people that worked to make this book. For example, everyone who worked on this book was paid at least a living wage. You can learn more at the Ontario Living Wage Network.

This book is also available as a Global Certified Accessible™ (GCA) ebook. ECW Press's ebooks are screen reader friendly and are built to meet the needs of those who are unable to read standard print due to blindness, low vision, dyslexia, or a physical disability.

The interior of this book is printed on Sustana Opaque™, which is made from 30% recycled fibres and processed chlorine-free.

FSC www.fsc.org MIX Paper | Supporting responsible forestry FSC® C016245

ECW's office is situated on land that was the traditional territory of many nations, including the Wendat, the Anishinaabeg, Haudenosaunee, Chippewa, Métis, and current treaty holders the Mississaugas of the Credit. In the 1880s, the land was developed as part of a growing community around St. Matthew's Anglican and other churches. Starting in the 1950s, our neighbourhood was transformed by immigrants fleeing the Vietnam War and Chinese Canadians dispossessed by the building of Nathan Phillips Square and the subsequent rise in real estate value in other Chinatowns. We are grateful to those who cared for the land before us and are proud to be working amidst this mix of cultures.

ecwpress.com